Miss Julie

August Strindberg (18-9-1912) was born in Stockholm and began writing plays in 1869. His first major play was *Master Olof*, written in 1872 but not performed for nine years. His other plays include *The Father* (1887), *Miss Julie* (1888), *Creditors* (1888), *To Damascus, Parts I and II* (1898), *A Dream Play* (1901) and *The Ghost Sonata* (1907).

David Eldridge was born in Romford, Greater London. His full-length plays include *Serving It Up* (Bush Theatre, London, 1996); *A Week with Tony* (Finborough Theatre, London, 1996); *Summer Begins* (National Theatre Studio and Donmar Warehouse, London, 1997); *Falling* (Hampstead Theatre, London, 1999); *Under the Blue Sky* (Royal Court Theatre, London, 2000, awarded the *Time Out* Live Award for Best New Play in the West End in 2001); *Festen* (Almeida and Lyric Hammersmith Theatres, London, 2004); *M.A.D.* (Bush Theatre, 2004); *Incomplete and Random Acts of Kindness* (Royal Court Theatre, 2005); a new version of Ibsen's *The Wild Duck* (Donmar Warehouse, 2005); *Market Boy* (National Theatre, 2006); a new version of Ibsen's *John Gabriel Borkman* (Donmar Warehouse, 2007); *Under the Blue Sky* (Duke of York's Theatre, London, 2008); an adaptation of Jean-Marie Besset's *Babylone* (Belgrade Theatre, Coventry, 2009); *A Thousand Stars Explode in the Sky*, co-written with Robert Holman and Simon Stephens (Lyric Hammersmith, 2010); a new version of Ibsen's *The Lady from the Sea* (Royal Exchange Theatre, Manchester, 2010); *The Knot of the Heart* (Almeida Theatre, London, 2011); *The Stock Da'wa* (Hampstead Theatre, London, 2011); and *In Basildon* (Royal Court Theatre, 2012).

Published by Methuen Drama, 2012

Methuen Drama, an imprint of Bloomsbury Publishing Plc

1 3 5 7 9 10 8 6 4 2

Methuen Drama
Bloomsbury Publishing Plc
50 Bedford Square
London WC1B 3DP
www.methuendrama.com

Copyright © David Eldridge 2012

David Eldridge has asserted his rights under the Copyright, Designs and Patents
Act, 1988, to be identified as the translator of this work

ISBN 978 1 408 17275 9

A CIP catalogue record for this book is available from the British Library

Available in the USA from Bloomsbury Academic & Professional,
175 Fifth Avenue/3rd Floor, New York, NY 10010.
www.BloomsburyAcademicUSA.com

Typeset by Mark Heslington Ltd, Scarborough, North Yorkshire
Printed and bound in Great Britain by CPI Group (UK) Ltd, Croydon, CR0 4YY

August Strindberg

Miss Julie

a version by

David Eldridge

from a literal translation by Charlotte Barslund

For Maxine

Methuen Drama

This version of *Miss Julie* was first performed at the Royal Exchange Theatre, Manchester on 11 April 2012. The cast was as follows:

Miss Julie	Maxine Peake
Jean	Joe Armstrong
Kristin	Carla Henry
Fiddler	Liam Gerrard
Ensemble	Cara Lee
	Cassandra John-Baptiste
	Victoria Pasion
	Anna Reilly
	Florence Rose King
	Jordana Wilson

Director   Sarah Frankcom
Designer   Max Jones
Lighting   Johanna Town
Sound   Steve Brown
Composer   Olly Fox
Dialects   Joe Windley
Company Manager   Lee Drinkwater
Stage Manager   Philip Hussey
Deputy Stage Manager   Jen Davey
Assistant Stage Manager   Simon Narciso
Fight Director   Kate Waters

Characters

Miss Julie
Jean, *the valet*
Kristin, *the cook*
Some other servants

The play takes place in the Count's kitchen on Midsummer's Night.

A large kitchen.

There are two shelves with copper, cast-iron and pewter pots and a large tiled stove with a hood. The stove is decorated with leafy birch branches and the floor is strewn with juniper twigs. There's an icebox, a draining board, a sink.

There's a white painted pine dining table surrounded by some chairs. A large Japanese spice jar with lilacs in bloom stands on it.

There are two arched glass doors through which a fountain with a cupid, flowering lilac bushes and tall poplars can be seen. There's a large, old-fashioned bell above another door with a speaking tube fixed on its left side.

Kristin *stands by the stove frying something in a pan. She is wearing a light-coloured cotton dress and an apron.*

Jean *enters dressed in livery and carrying a large pair of riding boots with spurs. He puts them down on the floor where they remain visible.*

Jean   Miss Julie's gone stark, raving mad again tonight. Completely mad.

Kristin   Is that you?

Jean   I took the Count to the station and on my way back I went in the barn. I went in to see what was going on and. You know. Perhaps, have a dance. There she is, Miss Julie, in front of everyone. Draped all over the gamekeeper. And then she claps her eyes on me. Comes right over. Arms round my waist and. Invites me. To do the ladies' waltz with her. And the way she danced. I've never seen anything like it. She is mad.

Kristin   She's always been mad. But you've got to admit it, the last fortnight's been something else. Since the engagement was broken off.

Jean   And what on earth was that all about? He was all right. Though I know he didn't have any money. These people. I don't know. If it's not one thing, it's something else.

He sits down at the end of the table.

Don't you think it's peculiar that a lady. Well. She'd rather stay at home with the staff, than go with her father and visit her relatives? At Midsummer.

Kristin   I expect she's embarrassed after all the business with her fiancé.

Jean   She probably is. But at least he was his own man in the end. Do you know what happened Kristin? I saw it you know. I saw all of it. Though I made out I didn't.

Kristin   You saw it?

Jean   Yes, Kristin, I did see it. They were in the stable yard the pair of them. It was this one evening. And Miss Julie was. Training him. That's what she called it. Do you know what she did? She made him jump over her riding crop. Like a dog. A dog. Twice. Twice he went over it and twice she smacked him. You know. Then the third time he had it out of her hand and broke it into little pieces. And that was when he left.

Kristin   With her riding crop?

Jean   Now darling, what have you got up your sleeve for me tonight?

Kristin *takes something out of the frying pan and sets the table for* **Jean**.

Kristin   A kidney. I had off of the veal.

Jean *smells the food.*

Jean   Wonderful. What a delicacy.

He touches the plate.

Kristin – the plate's cold.

Kristin   You're harder work than the Count you are.

She ruffles his hair affectionately.

Jean   Don't do that. You know I don't like it.

Kristin   I was only being tender. You know I am.

Jean *eats.* **Kristin** *opens a bottle of beer.*

Jean   Beer? On Midsummer? No, thank you, I can do better than that tonight.

He opens a drawer in the table and takes out a bottle of red wine sealed with yellow wax.

You see the yellow wax there? You see that seal? Get me a glass. Go on. A nice one. With a stem. Did you hear me?

Kristin *returns to the stove and puts a small pot on it.*

Kristin   God help the woman who marries you. You're so fussy.

Jean   Get out of it. You're dying to get your hands on me. And I bet you love it people go around calling me your fiancé as well.

He tastes the wine.

That's good. That's very good. Though it's a touch cold.

He warms the glass in his hand.

Picked it up in Dijon. Four francs for a litre before they bottled it, it was. And then there's the duty on top of that. What are you doing now? That smells disgusting.

Kristin   Oh it's right foul. Miss Julie wants it for Diana.

Jean   Right foul? Kristin, you've got to learn to express yourself in a more dignified manner. What are you cooking for her bitch on Midsummer for? Is it sick?

Kristin   It wandered off with the gatekeeper's dog and now she's bang in trouble. Miss Julie doesn't want any of that.

Jean   Miss Julie's so stuck-up about some things. And yet she's not got enough pride in herself about other things has she? Just like the late Countess. She was more happy than anyone whether she was in the kitchen or whether she was in the barn. And she'd never travel with just the one horse.

Her cuffs were grubby on occasion, but she had to have the coat of arms on all the buttons. But as for Miss Julie. She doesn't seem to look out for herself or her reputation at all at times. I'm half tempted to say she's not even a proper lady. Not a proper member of the aristocracy anyway. You know when she was dancing in the barn, she took the gamekeeper off of his Anna and didn't think twice about it. We'd never do anything like that would we? But you see when the aristocrats lower themselves like it then they go very low don't they? But you've got to give it to her, she's a handsome woman. Magnificent. The shoulders. The bearing. My God.

Kristin   Don't you get yourself too carried away she's nothing special. I've heard what Klara's got to say about her and she'd know, she dresses her.

Jean   Klara? Women are always so jealous of each other. I know what I'm talking about I've been out riding with her. And the way she danced.

Kristin   Will you dance with me Jean? When I've finished.

Jean   Of course I will.

Kristin   You promise you will?

Jean   When I say I will, then I will. Anyway, thank you for the kidney. It was delicious.

He puts the cork in the bottle.

Miss Julie *can be heard off.*

Miss Julie   I'll be back in a moment. Do carry on.

Jean *hides the bottle in the drawer and gets up respectfully.*

Miss Julie *enters and goes to* **Kristin** *at the stove.*

Miss Julie   So, have you done it for me?

Kristin *indicates that* **Jean** *is present.*

Jean   Perhaps the ladies have secrets they need to discuss in private?

Miss Julie *hits him in the face with her handkerchief.*

Miss Julie   That's for being nosy.

Jean   Lovely. Violets.

Miss Julie   Don't be so impertinent Jean. And you think you know about perfumery as well now do you? Well you certainly know how to dance I'll give you that. Go on, hop it, and no spying on us.

Jean   What is it a witches' brew you ladies are cooking up on Midsummer to tell a fortune? Make a wish on a star to show you your intended.

Miss Julie   If you can see that, then you must have good eyes, that's all I'll say.

To **Kristin**.

Pour it into a half bottle and make sure the cork's in properly. Jean, come and dance a Scottish reel with me.

Jean   I don't wish to be impertinent again Miss, but I promised the next dance to Kristin.

Miss Julie   She can have another later. Kristin would you mind me borrowing Jean please?

Kristin   If Miss Julie asks it's not for him to say no is it? He can go. And he should be grateful for it as well.

Jean   If I can speak plainly – and not wanting to hurt anyone's feelings. I don't think it's too clever for Miss Julie to dance with the same partner twice in a row. Because people are quick to jump to conclusions aren't they Miss?

Miss Julie   Jump to conclusions? What do you mean?

Jean   If Miss Julie doesn't want to take on board what I'm saying then I'll have to speak a bit more plainly. It looks bad to favour one servant over the others. Or they'll all expect the same treatment. Won't they?

Miss Julie   Favour one over the others? Well. I'm shocked, I must say. If the mistress of the house graces the servants' dance with her presence she wants a partner who can lead. And avoid looking completely ridiculous. That's all.

Jean   As Miss Julie wishes. Your word is my command.

Miss Julie   Don't say that I command you. Tonight we're all celebrating and happy. And as one. Give me your arm. Don't fret, Kristin. I won't take your fiancé away from you.

Jean *offers her his arm and escorts* **Miss Julie** *off.*

Kristin *thinks. Faint violin music from a Scottish reel can be heard in the distance.*

Kristin *hums along to the music and clears up after* **Jean**. *She washes the plate at the sink, dries it and puts it away in a cupboard.*

Then she takes off her cook's apron, takes out a small mirror from a drawer in the table, tilts it against the jar of lilacs on the table. She lights a candle and heats a hairpin with which she curls her fringe.

Then she goes to the door and listens. And returns again to the table. She finds **Miss Julie***'s handkerchief which she left behind and which she picks up and smells. Then she spreads it out, thinks, smooths it, stretches it and folds it four times.*

Jean *enters, alone.*

Jean   She really is mad. Dancing like that. People are laughing at her. Kristin?

Kristin   It's the curse. She's always like it when it's her time of the month. Will you dance with me?

Jean   Are you angry with me?

Kristin   No. I know my place.

Jean *puts his arms around her waist.*

Jean   Then you're a sensible girl, Kristin. You'll make someone a good wife.

Miss Julie *enters, unpleasantly surprised by what she sees.*

Miss Julie   Charming, abandoning a lady like that.

Jean   Miss Julie, you're not the one I abandoned.

Miss Julie *paces the kitchen.*

Miss Julie   No one dances quite like you. Did you know that? And why are you wearing that? It's Midsummer. Take it off. Now.

Jean   Miss Julie will have to excuse herself for a minute. You see my black coat's over there.

He moves towards it.

Miss Julie   Are you too shy to change in front of me? To change a jacket. Well go on go to your room if you must. And come back. Or shall I turn my back? I promise not to spy.

Jean   As you wish, my lady.

Jean *collects his coat and moves just out of the room to change.*

Miss Julie   Kristin, is Jean your fiancé? He's so at ease when he's in your company.

Kristin   Fiancé? If you like. It's what we say.

Miss Julie   What you say?

Kristin   Miss Julie's had a fiancé herself and knows –

Miss Julie   We were engaged to be married.

Kristin   And nothing came of it?

Jean *enters wearing a black coat and black hat.*

Miss Julie   *Très gentil, monsieur Jean. Très gentil.*

Jean   *Vous voulez plaisanter, madame.*

Miss Julie   *Et vous voulez parler français.* Where did you learn to speak like that?

Jean   In Switzerland. I was the sommelier at the biggest hotel in Lucerne.

Miss Julie   You look just like a gentleman. *Charmant.*

She sits down at the table.

Jean   You're flattering me Miss.

Miss Julie   Flattering you?

Jean   I'm a modest enough chap and I think to myself why would you exchange pleasantries with someone like me? And that's why I assumed you're flattering me.

Miss Julie   Where did you learn to speak like that? Are you often at the theatre?

Jean   I suppose I am.

Miss Julie   But you were born here? On the estate?

Jean   My father was a labourer on the Attorney's estate. Next door. I used to see Miss Julie when she was a girl. Though I don't think Miss Julie can ever have noticed me.

Miss Julie   Really?

Jean   And I remember once, one time in particular. Well, I shouldn't talk about it.

Miss Julie   Oh do. Please. Go on. Make an exception for me. Just this once.

Jean   No, I shouldn't really. Some other time.

Miss Julie   Another time may never come. Would it be so very. Naughty. To say it out loud?

Jean   No, it's not like that. I don't want to now. Look at her.

He indicates **Kristin** *has fallen asleep in a chair by the stove.*

Miss Julie   She'll make a cheerful enough wife. Does she snore?

Jean   No, but she talks in her sleep.

Miss Julie   How would you know she talks in her sleep?

Jean   Because I've heard her.

They watch each other intently. Silence.

Miss Julie   Why don't you sit down?

Jean I'm not allowed to sit down in your presence am I? Miss.

Miss Julie And what if I were to command you to?

Jean Then I would do as I was told.

Miss Julie Well sit down then. Wait. Get me something to drink first.

Jean I don't know what we've got in the icebox. There's only beer there.

Miss Julie I like beer. I think I prefer beer to wine.

Jean *takes a bottle of beer from the icebox, opens it, looks in the cupboard for a glass and a plate, then serves her.*

Jean There you go.

Miss Julie Thank you. Won't you have one?

Jean I don't like beer. But if Miss Julie tells me to.

Miss Julie I should think a gentleman should keep his lady company don't you?

Jean I think he should.

He opens another bottle and takes a glass.

Miss Julie Raise a toast to me. Now.

Jean *hesitates.*

Are you – shy?

Jean *gets on his knees, parodying in jest, and raises his glass.*

Jean To my mistress.

Miss Julie Bravo, bravo. Now kiss my foot. Go on. Do it. Now.

Jean *hesitates, but then grasps her foot gamely and kisses it lightly.*

Very good. You should have been an actor.

Jean *gets up.*

Jean   Someone might come in and see us.

Miss Julie   And what if they do?

Jean   People talk. It's as simple as that. And if Miss Julie only knew how some tongues are wagging already –

Miss Julie   Why? What did they say? What have they said? Tell me. Sit down.

Jean *sits down.*

Jean   I don't want to upset you, but they've cast a few aspersions. You know what I'm saying. You're not a girl and when people see an unmarried Lady drinking with a man at night – even though he's a servant. Then they –

Miss Julie   We're not alone. Kristin's here.

Jean   She's asleep.

Miss Julie   Then I'll wake her up.

Miss Julie *rises.*

Kristin. Are you sleeping?

Kristin   Now, now, now, now –

Miss Julie   Kristin? She knows how to sleep.

Kristin   Yes, the Count's boots have been done. And the coffee? Hurry up, hurry up, hurry – Now –

Miss Julie *pinches her nose.*

Miss Julie   Wake up –

Jean   Leave her she's sleeping.

Miss Julie   I beg your pardon?

Jean   She's been at the stove all day and she's tired when night time comes. Leave her be.

Miss Julie *paces.*

Miss Julie   How beautifully endearing. Well it does you great credit. Thank you.

She offers **Jean** *her hand.*

Now come with me. Perhaps we'll pick a lilac or two.

Silence.

Jean   With you? Picking lilacs?

Miss Julie   Yes, with me.

Jean   That won't do I'm afraid Miss. It absolutely won't do.

Miss Julie   What is it? Have you got something in your head?

Jean   But what about the other servants?

Miss Julie   What? Do you think I'm in love with the valet?

Jean   I wouldn't say I'm a conceited man. And I'm sure I'm not the first. But when the servants are. Well then nothing's sacred. Is it?

Miss Julie   I do believe I've an aristocrat before me.

Jean   Perhaps, I am.

Miss Julie   Then I lower myself.

Jean   No – Miss Julie. Listen to me. No one'll believe you chose to. People will always say you fell.

Miss Julie   I think, I think more highly of those people than you do. Come on. Now.

She looks at him willing him to her.

Jean   You're a strange one you are.

Miss Julie   Perhaps I am. And so are you. Everything's strange. Life is strange, people are strange, everything is an awful mess drifting, drifting on across the water until it sinks down. It all sinks. I have a recurring dream which often afflicts me. It comes to me now. I've climbed up to the top of a pillar and I don't see any way of getting down. And I feel dizzy when I look. Down I must, but I don't have the courage to throw myself from the pillar. I can't hold on for much longer and I long to fall. But I don't fall. And I will have no peace until I've fallen. No rest at all until I've come down, down to the very bottom. When I reach the ground I know I want to go down further. Sink even lower. The lowest of the low. Go into the earth itself. Have you ever felt anything like that?

Jean   I can't say I have. No, never. But I've often dreamt I'm lying under a tall tree. In a dark forest. I want to reach up and climb to the very top. Look out across the countryside. Where there's bright sunshine and it's warm. Rob a bird's nest for its golden eggs. And so I do climb up and up. But the trunk's so thick and slippery and it's so far to the first branch. I know that if I could reach the first branch then I could get all the way to the top. As if I was climbing a ladder. I haven't got there yet. But I will one day. Even if I only do it in my dreams.

Miss Julie   Here I am talking to you about dreams. With you. Come on. Let's go outside.

She offers him her arm and they begin to leave.

Jean   If we sleep on nine Midsummer flowers tonight, then our dreams will come true Miss Julie.

Miss Julie *and* **Jean** *turn around in the doorway.* **Jean** *touches his eye with one hand.*

Miss Julie   Let me see what's in your eye.

Jean   It's nothing. It's a fly. It's all right.

Miss Julie   It was the sleeve of my dress. I caught you. Sit down and let me look.

She takes his arm and sits him down. She pulls his head back and tries to remove the fly with the corner of her handkerchief.

Sit still. Absolutely still.

She slaps his hand.

Do as I say. I thought you were a big, strong man.

She feels his upper arm and then his torso.

And so you are.

Jean   Miss Julie.

Kristin *has woken up, staggers sleepily out to bed.*

Miss Julie   *Monsieur Jean.*

Jean   *Attention. Je ne suis qu'un homme.*

Miss Julie   Sit still. There. It's gone. Kiss my hand and say thank you.

Jean *gets up.*

Jean   Miss, listen to me. Now that Kristin's gone to bed – Please. Will you listen to me –

Miss Julie   First you have to kiss my hand.

Jean   Listen to me.

Miss Julie   Kiss my hand.

Jean   Well then on your head be it.

Miss Julie   Be what?

Jean   Are you a girl?

Miss Julie   No. Would you like me to be?

Jean   No, you're not, Miss Julie.

Miss Julie   And what are you?

Jean   I'm someone who –

Miss Julie   Who evidently thinks he's something of a catch? How incredibly conceited you are. You're no Don Juan. More like a Joseph. Yes, a little Joseph.

Jean   You think so do you?

Miss Julie   I think you are.

Jean *steps boldly forward intending to put his arms around her waist and kiss her.* **Miss Julie** *slaps him across the face.*

There.

Jean   Are you toying with me Miss? Or are you in earnest?

Miss Julie   I am in earnest.

Jean   And too much in earnest at that. You're far too reckless for my taste. I've had it playing your games. I want to go back to work. The Count needs his boots doing and it's long past midnight.

Miss Julie   Put the boots away.

Jean   I won't. It's what I'm here for and I want to do it. I've never thought of myself as your plaything and I won't be either. I think too much of myself for that to happen.

Miss Julie   You're proud.

Jean   Yes I am.

Miss Julie   Have you ever loved?

Jean   I wouldn't use that word. I'd say I've been fond of many girls in my time. And once I was sick to the stomach because I couldn't have someone I wanted. Sick to the stomach with it. It was like the Princes in the Arabian Nights. Who couldn't eat or drink for love.

Miss Julie   Who was she?

Silence.

Who was she?

Jean   You can't make me tell you.

Miss Julie   I ask you as an equal. As a – a friend. Who was she?

Jean   It was you.

Miss Julie   How funny.

Jean   It was ridiculous. I didn't want to tell you before, but now I do. Do you have any idea how it looks from down here? No, you don't. You're like the hawk or the falcon. You'll never know because you're up there somewhere. High in the sky. I lived in a cottage on the estate next door with

seven brothers and sisters. And a pig in a dank field.
Nothing grew. Not even a tree. But out of our window I
could see the wall of the park here. And the orchard beyond
it. The tops of the trees. I thought it was like the Garden of
Eden. And there were evil angels with swords that were on
fire standing guard. But all the same, like all the other boys,
I soon found out how to get to the tree of life. You despise
me now don't you?

Miss Julie   All the boys I've ever known scrumped
for apples.

Jean   All the same I know you despise me. It doesn't matter.
One time I went in to the vegetable garden with my mother
to weed the beds. With the onions. And next to the garden
was a Turkish pavilion. There were jasmine trees and it was
overgrown with honeysuckle. I didn't know what it was for.
But I'd never seen such a beautiful place. People came and
went and then one day the door was left wide open. So I
sneaked in and saw the walls covered with pictures of kings
and emperors. And there were red curtains with tassels
covering the windows. You know what I'm talking about.
The toilet. I –

He picks a lilac and holds it under **Miss Julie***'s nose.*

I'd never been inside the house. I'd never seen anything
except the church. But it – It was beautiful and no matter
how much my thoughts wandered, they always came back to.
It. There. And little by little the need grew inside me. One
day I will have to have the pleasure of it. *Enfin*. I sneaked in
there, and I saw what it was like and my imagination. It. But
then someone came. And there was only one way out. For
the Gentry like. But there was another way I saw I could go.
Through the pit. And I had no choice so I –

Miss Julie *takes the lilac and lets it drop on to the table.*

As soon as I was out of there, I ran through a hedge full of
raspberries, and across a field of strawberries and I ended
up in the rose garden. I saw a pink dress. And a pair of
white stockings.

Silence.

It was you. I hid amongst the weeds and thistles and got scratched to pieces. I was wet and I stank to high heaven but I watched you. The white stockings amongst the roses.

Silence.

I remember thinking a thief can go into Heaven and be with the angels. But even as he lives and breathes on God's earth, the labourer's boy can't go in the park and play with the Count's daughter.

Miss Julie   Don't you think any poor boy like you would have thought the same?

Jean   If he was poor – yes – of course he would. Of course.

Miss Julie   It must be such a miserable bore to be poor.

Jean   The dog lies on the Countess's sofa with his nose in her lap. The horse has his muzzle caressed by the Lady's hand. But the servant boy –

He paces.

Sometimes a man has a talent so he can get on in the world. But how often does that happen? Do you know what I did? I jumped in the mill stream with all my clothes on. And I was pulled out and beaten till I was red raw. The following week when my father and the rest of the family went to my grandmother's I swung staying at home. I washed myself with soap and warm water and I put on my Sunday best and I went to church. Where I would see you. I saw you there. And when I went home I was determined in my mind I wanted to die. But I wanted to die beautifully and comfortably. And without any pain. Then I remembered it's dangerous to sleep under an elder bush. And we had a big one which had just begun to flower. I ripped off all the flowers and I made a bed in the oat bin. Have you ever noticed how soft and smooth oats are? Like human skin to touch they are. I shut the lid and I nodded off. When I woke up I was very ill. But I didn't die. As you can see. I don't know what was I doing. I hadn't a hope in hell of succeeding. It was all futile. As futile as thinking I could belong to a different class.

Miss Julie   You speak with great charm. Did you go to school?

Jean   No but I've read a lot of novels and I've been to the theatre. And besides, I've heard the aristocrats converse and that's where I've learned the most.

Miss Julie   You snoop on us?

Jean   Of course I do. And the things I've heard as well. Next to the coachman. Or rowing the boat. Once I heard Miss Julie and a lady friend –

Miss Julie   Oh? And what did you hear?

Jean   I blushed. I thought to myself where did she learn about things like that. Perhaps, deep down, there's not so much of a big difference between people as you'd think.

Miss Julie   How dare you. I can assure you of one thing, we don't behave like you when we're engaged to be married.

Jean   Are you sure about that Miss Julie? Don't come the innocent with me.

Miss Julie   I gave my love to a scoundrel.

Jean   Women always say that. After the event.

Miss Julie   Always?

Jean   That's right. I've heard it said countless times.

Miss Julie   Really?

Jean   Today's just the same.

Miss Julie *gets up*.

Miss Julie   Be quiet now. I don't want to hear any more.

Jean   I'd like to go to bed. Now.

Miss Julie   Go to bed on Midsummer?

Jean   I don't feel like dancing with the rabble up there.

Miss Julie   Take the key for the boat and row me out on the lake. I want to see the sun rise.

Jean   Would you say that was wise Miss?

Miss Julie   Are you concerned for your reputation?

Jean   Well I'd rather not look completely ridiculous. Or be sacked without a reference just when I'm beginning to establish myself. And I've certain responsibilities. Towards Kristin. In particular.

Miss Julie   I see, it's Kristin.

Jean   Yes it is Kristin. You should take my advice and go upstairs and go to bed. Miss.

Miss Julie   Would you like me to do your bidding?

Jean   For your own sake. I beg of you. It's late and the tiredness makes you feel drunk and your head feels hot. Go to bed. They're coming to look for me. And if they find us here together, you're done for.

They hear the sound of the servants singing off.

The Servants   Two women came out of the wood
   Tridiridi-ralla tridiridi-ra.
And both of them up to no good
Tridiridi-ralla-la.
They'll carve up your shilling
Tridiridi-ralla – tridiridi-ra.
And share you for kissing
Tridiridi-ralla-la.
This garland I give you my lover
Tridiridi-ralla – tridiridi-ra.
But I've already taken another
Tridiridi-ralla-la.

Miss Julie   I know all the servants and people that work here and I love them. And they love me. Let them come here if they want to.

Jean   Miss Julie, they don't love you. They'll eat your food all right, but they spit it out straight afterwards. Trust me. Listen to them, listen, listen to what they're singing. No, no, don't listen.

Miss Julie   What are they singing?

Jean   It's a song about you and me. A vulgar song.

Miss Julie   Damn them. Damn them.

Jean   The mob always acts in a cowardly way. And when it's like that all you can do is go –

Miss Julie   Go where? We can't go anywhere. We can't go into Kristin's room.

Jean   There's my room. And needs must. Honestly, you can trust me, I'm your friend. Truly. Sincerely.

Miss Julie   And what if they come to your room?

Jean   I'll bolt the door and if they try to break it in, I'll shoot them. Come on. Now.

Miss Julie   Promise –

Jean   I swear.

Miss Julie *exits quickly.* **Jean** *follows quickly.*

Peasants come in, in festive clothing and with flowers in their hats, led by a fiddler. A barrel of beer and a bottle of schnapps decorated with greenery are placed on the table. Glasses are found. They drink. Then they form a circle and sing and dance the musical game 'Two women came out of the wood'.

The Servants   Two women came out of the wood
   Tridiridi-ralla tridiridi-ra.
   And both of them up to no good
   Tridiridi-ralla-la.
   They'll carve up your shilling
   Tridiridi-ralla – tridiridi-ra.
   And share you for kissing
   Tridiridi-ralla-la.

This garland I give you my lover
Tridiridi-ralla – tridiridi-ra.
But I've already taken another
Tridiridi-ralla-la.

When it is done they leave, singing as they go.

Miss Julie *enters on her own. She sees the mess in the kitchen and clasps her hands. She thinks and takes a powder puff and powders her face.* **Jean** *enters.*

Jean   You heard them. Do you still think you can stay here?

Miss Julie   No. I don't think I can. What are we going to do?

Jean   Go away. Far away.

Miss Julie   Where?

Jean   To Switzerland, the Italian lakes, I don't know. Have you ever been there?

Miss Julie   No. Is it beautiful there?

Jean   The summer lasts all year. And as for the oranges.

Miss Julie   But tell me, what will we do there?

Jean   I'll open a hotel. There'll be first-class service and first-class guests as well.

Miss Julie   A hotel?

Jean   That's the life. New faces, a new language to gabble in. Never an idle moment to grumble about or worry yourself about. You're never looking for something to do because the bell? It's ringing night and day. The train's sounding its whistle. The bus comes and goes. And the coins are rolling in. That's the life.

Miss Julie   And me?

Jean   The mistress of the establishment. Pride of place. With your looks and your sense of style it's bound to be a roaring success. Roaring. You'll be like the Queen of Sheba behind the desk. Staff running around twitching at the sound of the electric bell. Guests filing in and out to settle their bills. Trembling at the thought of the expense. But you'll always sweeten the sting with your pretty smile darling. Let's get away from here.

He takes a timetable from his pocket.

If we go now and we get the next train we'll be in Malmö at half past six. Hamburg twenty to nine tomorrow morning. Frankfurt – Basle – a day later. And on the Gotthard Line in Como in – let me think about it – three days. Three days.

Miss Julie   That's all very well Jean but. Give me courage. Tell me that you love me. Put your arms around me.

Jean   I want to. But I daren't. Not in this house. I love you. Don't doubt that. Do you doubt it, Miss Julie?

Miss Julie   Julie. Call me Julie now. There are no longer any barriers between us. Please. Julie.

Jean   I can't. There'll always be something between us as long as we're in this house. The past's got its grip on me. And the Count? To this day I've never met anyone I've so much respect for. I only need to look at his gloves lying on a chair to feel small. The bell goes and I'm up like a frightened mare. I can see his boots. Look at them. Standing there straight as his back. But me – I.

He kicks the boots.

It's always been there. The fear. Since I was a boy. But it will go. Once I'm in another country. A republic. Yes. The valet can grovel for me and put on my livery. I wasn't born to this. I've got something, me, and if only I can get a leg up and get hold of the first branch. Then you'll see me climb. Today I'm the valet. But next year I'll have my own hotel. And ten years after that I'll live off of my investments and go to Bucharest. Get myself decorated and perhaps. Perhaps. I may even end up a Count myself.

Miss Julie   How wonderful.

Jean   You can buy yourself a title there. And then you'll become a Countess after all.

Miss Julie   Why should I care for any of that? I'm leaving all that here. Say that you love me. Otherwise – Well. Otherwise what am I?

Jean   I'll say it to you a thousand times. And again later as well. But as for all these. Feelings. You'll have to turn that in or we'll have had it. We've got to be rational. Sensible about it.

He takes out a cigar, cuts it and lights it.

Now sit down there. I'll sit here. And we can talk as if nothing's happened.

Miss Julie   My God. Have you no feelings at all?

Jean   No feelings? Me? No one's as full of feeling as I am. I know how to conduct myself. That's all.

Miss Julie   Like when you kissed my foot?

Jean   Well, that was then and this is now. Now we've got other things to think about.

Miss Julie   Don't speak to me like that.

Jean   One folly's already been committed tonight, let's not have another one shall we? The Count could be here at any time. And we'll have to decide our fate well before then. Tell me, what do you think of going to Switzerland? Do you like my ideas?

Miss Julie   They seem fine. But they need money. Have you got any money at all? Anything at all?

He chews his cigar.

Jean   I've what I know. My accomplishments. I've some French, some German and Italian. That's investment enough so far as I'm concerned.

Miss Julie   But unfortunately your accomplishments won't buy you a railway ticket will they?

Jean That's why I'm on the lookout for a partner who can advance me some funds.

Miss Julie And where will you find a partner at such short notice?

Jean You'll find him. If you want to be with me.

Miss Julie I can't do that. And I own nothing myself.

Silence.

Jean Then I'm afraid it's all off.

Miss Julie It's all off?

Jean Things can stay as they are.

Miss Julie Do you think I'll stay under this roof as your whore? Do you think I'll have people point and sneer at me? Do you think I could look my father in the eye after all this? No. Take me away from here and from this humiliation and disgrace. Oh, what have I done, my God, my God.

She sobs.

Jean Don't start all that again. What have you done? The same as all the others. And long before you were on the scene.

She screams convulsively.

Miss Julie And now you despise me. I'm falling. I'm falling.

Jean That's it. Fall. Fall. And come to me when you're done. And I'll lift you up again.

Miss Julie What terrible things have driven me to you? The feeble to the strong. The falling to the rising? Or was it love? Is this love? Do you even know what love is?

Jean I do. Do you think I don't?

Miss Julie The words you speak. The thoughts you think.

Jean   It's what I'm like. Now don't be shy and don't act the lady now. We're as two peas in a pod. There, there, come on, my darling, I'll get you a drink.

He opens the drawer in the table and takes out the wine bottle and fills up two used wine glasses.

Miss Julie   Where did you get that wine from?

Jean   From the cellar.

Miss Julie   It's my father's burgundy.

Jean   Well it's good enough for his son-in-law then?

Miss Julie   I drink beer. I.

Jean   Well it just goes to show you've an inferior palate compared to me.

Miss Julie   You're no better than a common thief.

Jean   Oh you're not thinking of squealing are you?

Miss Julie   Oh, so I'm to be your accomplice am I? Am I completely drunk? Have I been dreaming? Yes that's it I'm dreaming – I'm sleep-walking through Midsummer. What innocent larks!

Jean   Innocent larks?

She paces up and down the room.

Miss Julie   Is there anyone on earth as unhappy as I am at this moment?

Jean   What have you got to be unhappy about? After managing to bag me. Think of Kristin. In there. Or perhaps you don't think she's got any feelings?

Miss Julie   I used to think so. But not any more. No. A servant's a servant.

Jean   And a whore's a whore.

She gets on her knees with folded hands.

Miss Julie God in Heaven, please put an end to my wretched life. Take me away from the filth into which I'm sinking. Save me! Save me oh Lord!

Jean I won't deny I feel sorry for you. When I was a boy. Lying there amongst the onions. When I saw you in the rose garden. Those white stockings. Then. I'll tell you something. I had exactly the same dirty thoughts as every other boy.

Miss Julie You, who would die for me?

Jean What, in the oat bin? Talk's cheap.

Miss Julie You were lying?

He yawns.

Jean I think I read a story in the newspaper once about a chimney sweep who laid himself down in a box of lilacs. Because he'd been told to pay up and support his child –

Miss Julie I see. So you're like that –

Jean I had to think of something. You always need a flowery story to get a woman.

Miss Julie Scoundrel.

Jean *Merde.*

Miss Julie Well now you've seen the hawk on its back –

Jean Oh, not only on its back – Or have you forgotten?

Miss Julie I was to be the first branch was I?

Jean Shame it was rotten –

Miss Julie I was to be the hotel sign?

Jean That's right. And me the hotel.

Miss Julie Fluttering my eyelashes at your guests and fiddling the books?

Jean I can do that myself all right.

Miss Julie How is it that a human soul can be so entirely steeped in filth?

Jean   You'll learn to clean it.

Miss Julie   Lackey! Servant! Stand up when I speak to you!

Jean   Lackey's slut. Servant's whore. Shut up and get out.
You come in here telling me that I'm filth? You would know.
I've never seen a woman of my kind behave like you did
tonight. Do you think any servant girl would throw herself at
a man like you did? Have you ever seen a girl of my class
offer herself like that? I've only ever seen that sort of thing
amongst the animals. And the fallen women.

Miss Julie   Go on. Lay your hands on me. Walk on me if
that's what you want. I deserve nothing else. I'm a wretched
creature, I know I am. Help me.

Jean   I won't deny I played my part. I wanted you. The
big prize. But do you think a man in my position would ever
have dared look at you without being invited to? I'm still
taken aback.

Miss Julie   And proud as well.

Jean   Why shouldn't I be? Though it was a bit too easy
really. It would have been better if you'd played harder
to get.

Miss Julie   Go on, why don't you hit me?

He gets up.

Jean   No. Forgive me. For what I've said. Please. I wouldn't
hit an unarmed man and certainly not a woman. I've come
to my senses. It was fool's gold and nothing else that's
blinded us down here.

Silence.

And to have seen for myself that the hawk's grey on its back.
And that those fine cheeks are well made up. That there's
grime under those manicured nails. That her handkerchief
was dirty. Though it smelled of perfume all right. It hurts
me to know. In my heart. That the thing I wanted more than

anything else. You. Is. That's all you are. To see you sunk
so low. Lower than your cook. I hurt the way I do when I
see the harvest ruined by a storm. In the end it's nothing
but dirt.

Miss Julie   You speak to me as if you already tower
above me.

Jean   I do. I could make you a Countess. But you can never
make me a Count.

Miss Julie   It's in my blood.

Jean   I could father a Count.

Miss Julie   Thief.

Jean   Thieving's not so bad. There's worse things you can
be in life. And by the way. I'm a part of this house and a part
of the family in this house. And it's not considered theft
when a member of the household plucks a berry from the
bush which has plenty.

His passion is aroused once more.

You're a remarkable woman Miss Julie. Far too good for
someone like me. You were drunk and you want to explain
your mistake away by making yourself believe you love me.
You don't love me. You desired me. You wanted me. And if
that's what it was then your love's no different than mine.
But I could never be happy as your piece of rough. And I
know I'll never be your true love.

Miss Julie   And you're quite sure of that are you?

Jean   Oh you'll say it could happen. That I should be able
to love you. Sure. Of course you will. You're beautiful. More
than that. You're magnificent.

He moves closer to her and takes her hand.

You're educated. Clever. Graceful and gracious when you
want to be. And once you've kindled a man's flame, it will
never die.

He puts his arms around her waist.

You intoxicate me. One kiss from you. And –

He attempts to lead her off, but she frees herself quietly.

Miss Julie   You won't get round me like that.

Jean   Not like that eh? Not a caress or a pretty word? Not by making a dream come true, or by saving you from disgrace either? Tell me how to then?

Miss Julie   How? How? How do I know? I despise you. As I despise the vermin that are also part of the household here. And as with the rats we can't rid ourselves of, there's no escape from you.

Jean   Then escape with me.

Miss Julie   Escape with you? I'm tired. Give me a glass of wine.

He pours the wine. She looks at her watch.

We should talk. We still have time.

She drinks all the wine and holds the glass out for more.

Jean   Don't drink so much. You'll get drunk.

Miss Julie   I don't care.

Jean   You don't care? It's common to get drunk.

Miss Julie   Escape. Yes. But we need to talk first. You've done all the talking and now it's my turn. You've told me about your life. But I want to tell you about mine. So we both know how low we both have sunk before we begin our journey on.

Jean   Think before you open your mouth.

Miss Julie   Are you my friend?

Jean   I suppose I am. But I wouldn't rely on me.

Miss Julie   Everyone knows my secrets anyway. My mother was a commoner. Very ordinary actually. She was brought up with all the ideas of her time. Equality, woman's

emancipation and that sort of thing. She had the most
pronounced aversion towards marriage. So of course when
my father proposed to her she said she could never be his
wife. But she told him he could be her lover. He explained to
her, he had no wish to see the woman he loved enjoying less
respect than he did. She said the respect of the world meant
nothing to her and spurred on by his own passion he agreed
to her terms. He was shunned by his own class and limited to
a domestic life. And of course it could never satisfy him. I
came into the world, though my mother never wanted
children. She wanted to rear me as a child of nature.
She wanted me to learn everything that a boy is taught. She
wanted me to become an example of how a woman could be
as good as a man. She put me in boy's clothes. Taught me to
handle the horses. But not to go in the barn. I had to groom
them and harness them. I learned about agriculture and
hunting. Even to slaughter cattle. It was vile. And all over
the estate men were told to do women's work and women to
do men's work. The estate went to pieces. We became a
laughing stock. Finally my father must have come to from
her spell and rebelled. Everything was changed back and
my parents were quietly married. It was then my mother fell
ill. I don't know what of. She had convulsions. She'd hide
away in the attic or the garden. Sometimes she stayed out
all night. Then there was the fire. The house, the stables
and the barn all burned to the ground. It was all very
dubious. Arson was suspected since the fire happened
the day after the insurance expired. Unfortunately the
renewal was delayed.

She fills the glass and drinks.

Jean   Don't drink any more.

Miss Julie   What does it matter? We stood on the bare
ground and slept in our carriages. My father didn't know
where he'd get the money to rebuild the house. Since he'd
neglected most of his old friends. Then my mother
suggested he try a childhood friend of hers. A brick

manufacturer who lived nearby. Father had a loan from him all right and he wasn't asked to pay any interest. Which surprised him and. The estate was rebuilt.

She drinks again.

Do you know who burnt down the estate?

Jean Your mother?

Miss Julie Do you know who the brick manufacturer was?

Jean Your mother's lover?

Miss Julie Do you know whose money it was?

Jean No, I don't know. I can't think.

Miss Julie My mother's.

Jean You mean it was the Count's own money? Unless they had some sort of agreement before they got married I suppose?

Miss Julie My mother had her own money. A small fortune actually. She didn't want my father to control it so her friend looked after it.

Jean I say.

Miss Julie My father found out, but he couldn't take him to court. He couldn't pay his wife's lover. He couldn't prove it was my mother's money. He wanted to shoot himself. Someone did once tell me he tried and failed. But he got over it. My mother paid for it though. For five long years.

Silence.

I loved my father. But because of his cruelty I instinctively took my mother's side. I didn't know what had happened then. Because of her I learned to hate men. She hated men. I swore to my mother I'd never become any man's slave.

Jean And then you got yourself engaged. To the County Attorney.

Miss Julie Yes. And he would be my slave.

Jean   Oh he didn't want that then?

Miss Julie   He wanted to but he bored me.

Jean   I saw you. In the stable yard.

Miss Julie   Really? What did you see?

Jean   I saw him break off the engagement.

Miss Julie   Well that's a lie. I broke it off. Has he said he broke it off, has he, the scoundrel?

Jean   He's no scoundrel, he was all right. Miss Julie, you hate men.

Miss Julie   Yes I do. Most of the time. But sometimes. A weakness comes over me. Oh my.

Jean   You hate me as well?

Miss Julie   Very much. I'd like to kill you. Like a dog.

Jean   'The offender is sentenced to two years' hard labour and his dog's to be put down.' Isn't that how it goes Miss Julie?

Miss Julie   Just like that.

Jean   But there's no prosecutor. No sign of a dog. What are we going to do?

Miss Julie   Go abroad.

Jean   And torment each other to death?

Miss Julie   No. We should enjoy ourselves for as long as we can. Two days. Eight days. Who knows? Then we die.

Jean   Die? I think we might be better off in the hotel trade.

Miss Julie   Yes, to die by Lake Como. Where the sun's always shining. The laurels are green at Christmas time. And the oranges glow like the sun.

Jean   Lake Como's a rainy piss hole at the best of times and the only oranges I saw were in the market. It's a good place for tourists though. Villas for lovers and all that. There's a profitable trade to be had. And do you know why? They sign a six-month contract but they're gone after three weeks.

Miss Julie   Why?

Jean   They fall out. But the rent has to be paid all the same. Then you let it out again. And on it goes. Because there's always plenty of eloping lovers knocking about. Even if the love doesn't last very long.

Miss Julie   Don't you want to die with me?

Jean   No. I don't want to die. I enjoy being alive. And suicide's a sin against God.

Miss Julie   Oh you believe in God?

Jean   Of course I do. And I go to church every other Sunday as well. I'm tired of all this now. I'm going to bed.

Miss Julie   You think you can brush me off just like that? You owe me.

He takes his wallet and throws a silver coin on the table.

Jean   There. I don't like to be in hock to anyone.

Miss Julie   Do you know what the law says?

Jean   What? Regarding a woman seducing a man? No law exists. Miss.

Miss Julie   Do you see any other way out of this other than us going away, getting married and then separating?

Jean   And what if I'm reluctant to enter into a misalliance?

Miss Julie   A misalliance?

Jean   There's no arsonists in my family.

Miss Julie   I wouldn't be so sure.

Jean   There's no records of my family. Except criminal records I expect. But I've been in the library and studied your family history. Do you know about the miller whose wife the King slept with? While we were at war with Denmark as well.

Miss Julie   So this is what I get for opening my heart to an undeserving wretch? For sacrificing my family's honour?

Jean   You shouldn't drink because you start talking. And then you don't know when to shut your mouth.

Miss Julie   How I regret it all. How I regret it. If only you loved me.

Jean   What do you mean? What do you want me to do? Cry? Do you want me to jump over your riding crop? Shall I kiss you? Trick you into going to Lake Como with me for three weeks, and then say goodbye? What shall I do? What will you do? This is all too much for me now. This is what happens when a man sticks his nose into women's business, Miss Julie. I can see you're miserable. I know you suffer. But I don't understand you. We're not like you. There's none of this to do amongst folk of my class. Love's a game you play when you're not at work. Fortunately we don't have all day and all night like you do. You're sick. Your mother was sick. And I've heard there's whole towns and villages being corrupted by the sickness of your class. Spread by silly ideas in books I'm sure.

Miss Julie   You must feel something. You're talking like a human being. Now.

Jean   And yet you'd spit on me and you wouldn't let me wipe myself on you neither.

Miss Julie   Help me. Help me. Tell me what to do? What shall I do?

Jean   Jesus wept. I don't know.

Miss Julie   I know I've been absurd. But surely there must be some way I can save myself.

Jean   No one knows anything.

Miss Julie   Impossible. Those people knew and Kristin knows.

Jean   They don't. They couldn't even fathom it.

Miss Julie   But it could happen again.

Jean   I suppose it could.

Miss Julie   And what then?

Jean   What then? I can't even think straight. There's only one thing you can do. Leave. Right away. I won't be able to come with you because then everything will be lost. You've got to go on your own. Go anywhere.

Miss Julie   Anywhere? Alone? I can't do that.

Jean   You've got to. And before the Count comes back as well. If you stay here, we both know what will happen. We'll go on – and on. Getting more and more careless. And eventually you'll be found out. Go. Write to the Count and confess to him. But don't you say that it was me. He'll never guess it was me. He won't want to know who it was anyway.

Miss Julie   I'll go if you come with me.

Jean   Are you mad, Miss Julie? You want to run away with your valet? It will be all over the papers by the day after tomorrow. And the Count will never get over that.

Miss Julie   I can't leave. I can't stay. Help me. I'm so tired, so tired. Tell me what to do. Set me on in one direction or the other. Because I can't think any more. I can't do anything any more.

Jean   What peculiar little creatures you are. You puff yourselves up and stick your noses in the air as if you were the very lords of creation. I'll tell you. Go upstairs and get dressed. Get some money to take with you and then come back downstairs.

Miss Julie   Come with me upstairs.

Jean   To your room? Are you mad?

Silence.

No. Go on. Now.

He takes her hand and leads her off.

Miss Julie   Please be kind to me.

Jean   An order always sounds unkind. Now you know. Now you know.

She goes. He is on his own. He heaves a sigh of relief and sits down by the table. He takes out a notebook and a pencil and calculates mumbling something out loud.

Kristin *enters dressed for church holding a shirt in front of her and a white tie in her hand.*

Kristin   Jesus, Mary and Joseph, what a mess. What have you been up to?

Jean   Miss Julie dragged in the rest of the staff. Didn't you hear anything?

Kristin   I slept like a log.

Jean   And you're dressed for church already?

Kristin   You promised to take communion with me today.

Jean   I did. And you've brought my Sunday best an' all?

He sits down. **Kristin** *starts to dress him in the shirt front and white tie. Silence.*

What's the gospel preached today?

Kristin   The one when John the Baptist gets his head cut off.

Jean   It's too tight, you're choking me. Oh, I'm so tired, I'm dog tired.

Kristin   What have you been doing up all night? You look green around the gills.

Jean   I've been sitting here talking to Miss Julie.

Kristin   That woman doesn't know what's proper and what's not proper.

Silence.

Jean   Kristin.

Kristin   What?

Jean   Don't you think it's odd to think about it. Her.

Kristin   What's odd?

Jean   Everything.

Silence.

Kristin *looks at the half-empty glasses standing on the table.*

Kristin   Have you been drinking with her as well?

Jean   Yes.

Kristin   Look me in the eye.

Jean   What?

Kristin   Did you? Did you?

Silence.

Jean   Yes. I did.

Kristin   I would never have believed that. No, damn you. Damn you, you bastard.

Jean   You're not jealous of her are you?

Kristin   No, not of her. No. If it had been Klara or Sofi I would have scratched your eyes out. But her? I don't know why I. It's disgusting.

Jean   Are you angry with her?

Kristin   I am with you. It was wrong. You shouldn't have done it. It was wrong. Both of you. I don't want to be in a house where I can't respect my betters.

Jean   Why should you have to respect them?

Kristin   Why don't you tell me? You that knows it all. Do you want to serve people who carry on like it? Eh? It's indecent. We'll all be tarred with the same brush.

Jean   Don't you like to know they're no better than us?

Kristin No I don't. Because if they're no better than us then what's it worth striving for to become a better person? And think of the poor Count. He's endured so much grief in his time. Lord have mercy. I don't want to be in this house any more. And with you as well. If it had been someone of her own class then –

Jean Then what?

Kristin I'll never forget this with Miss Julie. Miss Julie who was so proud. So rotten towards all men. You'd never think that she'd give herself over to someone like you. To think she wanted the bitch shooting for running after the gatekeeper's dog. I'll have my say all right. But I'm not staying here any longer than my notice and on the twenty-fourth of October I'll be gone.

Jean And then what?

Kristin It's about time you started looking for something else. Seeing as we intend to get married.

Jean I can't get a job like this as a married man.

Kristin Then you'll have to look for a job as a caretaker. Or a porter. Won't you? In a government department. The pay's not much, but they're safe jobs. And they come with a pension. You've got to think of your wife. And the children.

Jean I might as well pack in now. I must confess darling that I did have slightly higher ambitions in life.

Kristin Ambitions? You've responsibilities. And you should think about those.

Jean Don't you start talking to me about responsibilities. I know what I've got to do.

He listens for something.

There'll be plenty of time to think about all that later. Now go and get yourself ready for church.

Kristin Who's that wandering about upstairs?

Jean   I don't know. Perhaps it's Klara.

Kristin   It's not the Count is it? He wouldn't have come home without anyone hearing him would he?

Jean thinks.

Jean   The Count? No, he would have rung for me.

Kristin   God help us, I never thought I'd be mixed up with this sort of trouble.

She goes. He notices the sun has risen and lights up the top of the trees in the park. The shadows cast by the onset of dawn begin to move slowly until sunshine spills through the windows. He goes to the door and makes a sign.

Miss Julie *enters in travelling clothes carrying a small birdcage covered with a towel which she places on a chair.*

Miss Julie   I'm ready now.

Jean   Be quiet. Kristin's awake.

Miss Julie   Does she suspect?

Jean   She doesn't know anything. Look at you.

Miss Julie   What? How do I look?

Jean   You like you've just been dug up. And what's that muck on your face?

Miss Julie   Let me wash it off.

She goes to the washing bowl and washes her face and hands.

There. See. Give me a towel. The sun's up.

Jean   Yes it is. And the power of the troll is broken.

Miss Julie   Listen to me Jean. Come with me. I've the money now.

Jean   But is it enough money?

Miss Julie   Enough to begin with. Come with me. I can't go on my own. Not today. Midsummer's Day on a stuffy, packed train. All those people staring at me. Stopping at every station when really I want to flee and be gone. I can't do it, I can't. And then I'll remember. Midsummer's Days as a girl. At church garlanded with leaves and twigs. Birch and lilacs. Dinner with friends and family. Afternoons in the park. Dancing. Music. Flowers. Games. One can run, but the memories will always follow you. With the luggage. You remember. You feel awful. Your conscience – It.

Jean I'll come with you. Now. Before it's too late. This minute.

Miss Julie Well, get dressed then.

Miss Julie *takes the birdcage.*

Jean No bags. No luggage. We'll be found out.

Miss Julie I've only brought what will go in the compartment.

Jean *takes his hat.*

Jean What have you got there? What's that?

Miss Julie It's only my Serine. I can't leave her behind.

Jean Oh so we're taking that are we? You're mad you are. Leave it.

Miss Julie It's the only thing I'm taking. It's the only thing that loves me. I've not even got Diana. Even she betrayed me. Don't be so horrid. I want it.

Jean Keep your voice down, Kristin will hear.

Miss Julie I won't leave it with a stranger. I'd rather it were dead.

Jean Give me it here and I'll wring its neck.

Miss Julie Don't hurt it. Don't – No. I can't.

Jean Give it here and I'll do it.

Miss Julie *takes the bird out of the cage and kisses it.*

Miss Julie My little Serine. Must you die? And go and leave your mistress now as well?

Jean   It's for your own good.

He takes the bird from her, goes to the chopping block and takes the kitchen axe. **Miss Julie** *turns away.*

You should have learned what to do with a chicken rather than bothering shooting guns –

He chops. She screams.

Then you wouldn't be so faint at the sight of a drop of blood.

Miss Julie   Kill me. Kill me please. To think you could kill an innocent creature without your hand even shaking. I hate and despise you. Blood's spilt now. I curse the moment I saw you. I curse the very moment I was conceived in my mother's womb.

Jean   Cursing won't help you. Come on.

She approaches the chopping block as if drawn against her will.

Miss Julie   I don't want to leave yet. I can't – I have to see. Hush, that's a carriage coming up the drive.

She listens all the while keeping her eyes fixed on the block and the axe.

You think I can't stand the sight of blood. You think I'm weak? I'd like to see you bleed. Your brains splattered all over a chopping block. I'd like to see all men. All the creatures of your sex swimming in a lake of blood. I would drink from your skull. Wash my feet in your ribcage. And eat your heart. Roast it. You think that I'm weak? You think that I love you and that my body desires your. Seed. You think I'll carry your child beneath my own heart and nourish it with my own blood. Bear your child and take your name? What's your name again? I've never heard it. I don't suppose you've got one of your own. I would become Mrs Gatekeeper. Mrs Valet. Mrs Below-Stairs. Your dog wear my collar? A labourer's son wear my crest on your buttons? That I should share you with my cook? Be the rival of my servant? Really? Really? You think that I'm a coward who wants to flee? No, no, no I'll stay here and what will be will be. My father will return and find his desk broken into and his money gone. Then he'll ring and ring that bell. Twice for his valet. He'll send for the police. And then I'll tell him everything. Everything. Oh to put an end to it all. If only it was the end. His heart will break and then he'll die. And that will be the end for all of us. Everything will be quiet. There will be enough peace to last an eternity. The coat of arms will be broken over his coffin. The Count's line at an end and the valet's line going forth in an orphanage. Garnering its laurels in the gutter and ending up in prison I'm sure.

Jean   Bravo, Miss Julie, there's a blue blood. But give over now will you?

Kristin *enters dressed for church with a hymn book in her hand.*
Miss Julie *rushes towards her and falls into her arms as if seeking protection.*

Miss Julie   Help me, Kristin. Help me against this man.

Kristin   What's all this on a Sunday morning?

Kristin *notices the chopping block.*

What's all this mess? What are you screaming and carrying on like this for?

Miss Julie   Kristin. You're a woman. And you're a dear friend. Watch out for that scoundrel.

Jean   While you ladies are conversing I think I'll go and shave.

He slips out of the room.

Miss Julie   Now, you must listen to me.

Kristin   Where are you going, Miss? You're in your travelling clothes? And him wearing his hat as well?

Miss Julie   Listen to me, Kristin, listen to me and I'll tell you everything –

Kristin   I'd rather you didn't –

Miss Julie   Listen to me –

Kristin   What's all this about? Is it this silly business with Jean? Well, if it is, I'll tell you this, I don't care much for it. It doesn't mean anything to me. But if Miss Julie's thinking of running off with him, then I'm not having that.

Miss Julie   Kristin, listen to me. Please be calm. I can't stay here and Jean can't stay here. So we have to go.

Kristin   Oh.

Miss Julie   But you see, I've had an idea. The three of us can go. To Switzerland. We can open a hotel together. I've got the money. Jean and I would take care of everything. And I thought. You could be in charge of the kitchen. Doesn't that sound marvellous? Say yes. Please. Come with us. Everything will be fine then. Do please say yes.

Miss Julie *embraces* **Kristin** *and pats her on the back.*

Kristin   Right.

Miss Julie   You've never travelled have you Kristin? You should get out and see the world. You can't imagine what fun it is to travel by train. You meet new people and see new countries. We'll stop in Hamburg and visit the Zoo. You'll like that. We'll go to the theatre. The opera. In Munich the museums are just splendid. You'll see. Rubens and Raphael. All the greats. You have heard about Munich? It's where King Ludwig lived. You know the one who went mad. We can go to his castle. Exactly like in all the fairy tales. And then Switzerland. It's not too far. The Alps. With snow on top of them as well. In the middle of summer. Oranges. Like the – And laurels that are green all year round.

Jean *hovers sharpening his razor on a strap which he holds with his teeth. He listens to the conversation with a pleased expression and nods with approval in places.*

And we'll open a hotel. I'll mind the desk and Jean will welcome the guests. We'll go shopping. Write letters. That's the life. The train whistling, the bus coming and going, the bell ringing upstairs, the bell ringing in the restaurant. I'll write out the bills. Ensure they settle without complaint. And you? You'll be in the kitchen. Of course you won't be slaving over the stove. You'll be in charge. And well turned out. You'll be meeting people. And with your looks. I'm not flattering you. You'll find yourself a husband one day. A rich Englishman. English men are so easy to – bag. We'll be rich. And build ourselves a villa at Lake Como. Of course it rains. Sometimes. But I'm assured the sun does put in an appearance once in a while. Just when you think it's all gloom and doom. And. Then. Otherwise – I suppose we can just go back home again. And come back.

Silence.

Here. Or somewhere else.

Kristin   Give over, you don't even believe it yourself.

Miss Julie   I don't believe it?

Kristin   That's right.

Silence.

Miss Julie   I don't believe in anything any more.

She collapses on the bench, drops her head between her arms on the table.

Nothing. Nothing at all.

Kristin *turns and looks at* **Jean** *hovering half in the room.*

Kristin   So you're thinking of running off?

He puts the razor down on the table.

Jean   Running off? That's a bit of an exaggeration. You heard Miss Julie. I know she's tired and emotional. She's been up all night. But it could still happen.

Kristin   Get out of it. And me your cook an' all eh?

Jean   Mind your tongue when you're speaking to your mistress. You hear me?

Kristin   Mistress?

Jean   Yes.

Kristin   I say, listen to him.

Jean   No, you listen, you listen. You want to shut your mouth and open your ears. Miss Julie's your mistress. You despise her now, but you should despise yourself for much the same.

Kristin   I've always respected myself I know that much.

Jean   But you despise other people all the same.

Kristin   I never lowered myself like her I know that. It would be like me carrying on with one of the Count's swine.

Jean   But you're all right, you've been carrying on with someone half decent.

Kristin   So half decent he sells oats from the Count's stables.

Jean   You can talk. You and your cut from the grocer –

Kristin   What?

Jean   You've no respect.

Kristin   Are you coming to church or not? I think you're the one who could do with a good sermon this morning.

Jean   I'm not going to church today. You'll have to go by yourself. You can confess your sins.

Kristin   I will. And you better hope I come home with enough forgiveness in me for the two of us. The Lord Jesus Christ died on the cross for all our sins. And if we seek forgiveness and repent he will bear them for us.

Jean   I hope he's willing to take the groceries.

Miss Julie   Do you truly believe Kristin?

Kristin   It's what I believe and what I've always believed, Miss Julie. Where there's sin there's grace as well.

Miss Julie   If only I had your faith.

Kristin   Well you're not having anything that's mine. It's God's will.

Miss Julie   God's will?

Kristin   God favours no one, except that, the last shall be the first.

Miss Julie   He favours the last?

Kristin   It's easier for a camel to pass through the eye of a needle than for a rich man to enter the kingdom of Heaven. That's just the way it is, Miss Julie. Sorry. I'm going now and I'll make sure to tell the stable boy not to hand over any horses. In case anyone tries to leave before the Count comes home.

Kristin *goes.*

Jean   And all over a dead bird.

Miss Julie   Don't you dare. Do you see an end to all this?

Jean   No.

Miss Julie   What would you do if you were me?

Jean   If I were you? I don't know. I haven't a clue. Perhaps I do.

Miss Julie *takes the razor and makes a gesture.*

Miss Julie   Would you do this?

Jean   Perhaps I would. No I wouldn't. That's the difference between us.

Miss Julie   Because you're a man and I'm a woman?

Jean   No.

Miss Julie *toys with the razor in her hand.*

Miss Julie   I want to. But I can't. My father couldn't do it either. And he should have done it.

Jean   No, but he had to get his revenge in first.

Miss Julie   And now Mother's avenged. Through me.

Jean   Have you ever loved your father, Miss Julie?

Miss Julie   Yes. More than anything. But I've hated him too I think. I must have done. He brought me up to hate my own sex. Half a woman and half a man. And who's to blame for that? My father? My mother? Myself? Am I to blame? I have nothing which is my own. I haven't an original thought in my mind that didn't come from my father. Not a passion in my heart that didn't come from my mother. And as for all that rot about all people being equal? Well that was my fiancé. The scoundrel. How can it all be my own fault? Should I blame God like Kristin does? No I'm too proud. Too clever by half. Thanks to my father. And as for all that business that a rich man cannot enter the kingdom of Heaven? That's a lie. And from Kristin. She's money saved and she won't get in to heaven anyway. Who is to blame? What does it matter? In the end I'm the only one who will be blamed. And it will be me to suffer the consequences.

Jean   But.

The bell rings sharply twice. **Miss Julie** *leaps to her feet.* **Jean** *changes his coat.*

The Count is here. Imagine if Kristin was to –

He goes to the speaking tube, taps it and listens.

Miss Julie   He's been to his desk hasn't he?

Jean   It's Jean. Sir.

He listens.

Yes, Sir.

Still listening.

Yes, Sir. Right away.

Still listening.

At once, Sir.

Still listening.

Yes. In half an hour.

Miss Julie   What did he say? Lord in Heaven above, tell me what did he say?

Jean   He wants his boots and his coffee in half an hour.

Miss Julie   So in half an hour I. I'm so tired. I can't do anything. I can't try to make amends, I can't run away, I can't stay. I can't live. I can't die. Help me. Tell me what to do. Command me. I'll do your bidding like a dog. Do me that one last favour. Save my honour. Save his name. You know what I'd like to do. But I can't. Be my will. Now.

Jean   I can't now. I don't know why. I don't understand it. It's as if my livery's made me everything I am. That's the best way I can put it – now. I can't give you orders. And now the Count's spoken to me. That's it. I can't explain myself properly. The devil's on my back. If the Count were to come down here now and order me to cut my throat I'd do it on the spot.

Miss Julie   Then pretend that you're him and I'm you. You act very well. You were on your knees. You were noble. An aristocrat. Or was that all a lie? And you've never been to the theatre. Never seen a hypnotist.

Jean *indicates that he has.*

He says take the broom. He takes it. He says sweep. And he sweeps –

Jean   You would have to be asleep.

Miss Julie   I'm already asleep. The whole room's filled with smoke. You look like an iron stove. That looks like a man dressed in black wearing a top hat. And his eyes burn. Like embers in a dying fire. Skin white as ash.

The sunlight begins to bathe **Jean** *in a warm glow.*

It's so very warm. And good.

She rubs her hands as if warming them in front of a fire.

So light. So peaceful.

Jean *takes the razor and puts it in her hand.*

Jean   Here's the broom. Now go to the barn while it's light.

He whispers in her ear.

Miss Julie   Thank you. Now I will rest. But tell me. The first may receive the gift of grace? Tell me. Even if you don't believe a word of it.

Jean   The first? Miss Julie. You're no longer among the first. You're among the last now.

Miss Julie   Yes I am. I'm among the last. I'm the last. I can't go now. Tell me to go once more.

Jean   No, I can't either. I can't either now.

Miss Julie   And the first shall be the last.

Jean   Don't think about it. Just don't think about it. You're sapping every ounce of strength I've got here. You're making a coward of me. Was that the bell? No. Shall we put some paper in it? Fancy me being so scared of the bell. But it's not the bell is it? It's him. It's his hand. Put your hands over your ears. Just put your hands over your ears. That's it. But then he'll just ring louder and he'll keep ringing until you answer it. And then it'll be too late. And then the police will be here. And then.

The bell rings twice, louder. **Jean** *is startled and then straightens himself.*

It's terrible. But there's nothing else to be done. Go on. Now.

Miss Julie *goes out through the door. Determined.*

End.

Methuen Drama Modern Plays

include work by

Edward Albee
Jean Anouilh
John Arden
Margaretta D'Arcy
Peter Barnes
Sebastian Barry
Brendan Behan
Dermot Bolger
Edward Bond
Bertolt Brecht
Howard Brenton
Anthony Burgess
Simon Burke
Jim Cartwright
Caryl Churchill
Complicite
Noël Coward
Lucinda Coxon
Sarah Daniels
Nick Darke
Nick Dear
Shelagh Delaney
David Edgar
David Eldridge
Dario Fo
Michael Frayn
John Godber
Paul Godfrey
David Greig
John Guare
Peter Handke
David Harrower
Jonathan Harvey
Iain Heggie
Declan Hughes
Terry Johnson
Sarah Kane
Charlotte Keatley
Barrie Keeffe

Howard Korder
Robert Lepage
Doug Lucie
Martin McDonagh
John McGrath
Terrence McNally
David Mamet
Patrick Marber
Arthur Miller
Mtwa, Ngema & Simon
Tom Murphy
Phyllis Nagy
Peter Nichols
Sean O'Brien
Joseph O'Connor
Joe Orton
Louise Page
Joe Penhall
Luigi Pirandello
Stephen Poliakoff
Franca Rame
Mark Ravenhill
Philip Ridley
Reginald Rose
Willy Russell
Jean-Paul Sartre
Sam Shepard
Wole Soyinka
Simon Stephens
Shelagh Stephenson
Peter Straughan
C. P. Taylor
Theatre Workshop
Sue Townsend
Judy Upton
Timberlake Wertenbaker
Roy Williams
Snoo Wilson
Victoria Wood

Methuen Drama Contemporary Dramatists

include

John Arden (two volumes)
Arden & D'Arcy
Peter Barnes (three volumes)
Sebastian Barry
Dermot Bolger
Edward Bond (eight volumes)
Howard Brenton
(two volumes)
Richard Cameron
Jim Cartwright
Caryl Churchill (two volumes)
Sarah Daniels (two volumes)
Nick Darke
David Edgar (three volumes)
David Eldridge
Ben Elton
Dario Fo (two volumes)
Michael Frayn (three volumes)
David Greig
John Godber (four volumes)
Paul Godfrey
John Guare
Lee Hall (two volumes)
Peter Handke
Jonathan Harvey
(two volumes)
Declan Hughes
Terry Johnson (three volumes)
Sarah Kane
Barrie Keeffe
Bernard-Marie Koltès
(two volumes)
Franz Xaver Kroetz
David Lan
Bryony Lavery
Deborah Levy
Doug Lucie

David Mamet (four volumes)
Martin McDonagh
Duncan McLean
Anthony Minghella
(two volumes)
Tom Murphy (six volumes)
Phyllis Nagy
Anthony Neilsen (two volumes)
Philip Osment
Gary Owen
Louise Page
Stewart Parker (two volumes)
Joe Penhall (two volumes)
Stephen Poliakoff
(three volumes)
David Rabe (two volumes)
Mark Ravenhill (two volumes)
Christina Reid
Philip Ridley
Willy Russell
Eric-Emmanuel Schmitt
Ntozake Shange
Sam Shepard (two volumes)
Wole Soyinka (two volumes)
Simon Stephens (two volumes)
Shelagh Stephenson
David Storey (three volumes)
Sue Townsend
Judy Upton
Michel Vinaver
(two volumes)
Arnold Wesker (two volumes)
Michael Wilcox
Roy Williams (three volumes)
Snoo Wilson (two volumes)
David Wood (two volumes)
Victoria Wood

For a complete catalogue
of Methuen Drama titles
write to:

Methuen Drama
Bloomsbury Publishing Plc
50 Bedford Square
London WC1B 3DP

or you can visit our website at:

www.methuendrama.com